Atmosphere Is Ours

Parker Schuchart

BookLeaf
Publishing

India | USA | UK

Made with ❤ on the BookLeaf Publishing Platform
www.bookleafpub.in
www.bookleafpub.com

Dedication

For you, who has taught me everything I know. Thank
you.

Preface

From a childhood shaped by fear
to an adulthood shaped by the hard work
of learning to feel without drowning.
This is what I am.

Acknowledgements

This collection was written in the spaces between—
between relationships, between identities, between
breaths.

Thank you to everyone who waited with me in those
spaces:

To my closest circle, who read these poems when they
were still raw and unfinished.

To my family, who gave me the first languages of fear
and love.

To the people these poems are about.

To the person I was becoming while writing them, who
I'm still learning to know.

And to you, reading this right now. Thank you for
making space for these words.

1. 2009

The garden hose water
always tasted like rubber and sun,
metallic and warm
even when you let it run.

I was always scared to drink it.
I was always scared to do anything.

I'd lie in the grass in my backyard
and stare at the sky.
Grass always made me itchy—
the same way my dry skin in the winter did.

My sister and I would spend all day
on the rope swing our father made,
she'd pump her legs fearlessly
while I dragged mine through the dirt.
I was always scared to go high.
I was scared until I wasn't.

The sound of ice cubes
cracking in water poured
from our sink,
bare feet on wood paneling,

the distant hum of the TV
from another room,
the long hallway,
our basement,
the height of doorknobs, the weight of the screen door
that took both hands to open.

My house always felt so big,

And my mother's hands always
looked so strong cutting
vegetables into a metal bowl,
the knife quick and sure,
the thunk of her blade on the cutting board.

The afternoon would stretch out after that.
I loved that specific quiet
between lunch and dinner,
when everything felt so safe,
so distant.

The whole world seemed to be napping,
and nothing needed to mean anything
beyond exactly what it was.

2. Father

Take the breath from out my chest,
For I know nothing but fear.
   Lying here—
         I whisper,
      "Father, please tell me when it's over."

3. Mother

My mother took me to the river
to wash the sins her father made her bear.

She set me down lightly,

relinquishing her guilt,
and gave me dirt to wear.

4. Check List

Shoes Clothes Wallet Keys the things that prove I existed Toothbrush Food Friends Family Soul all the Hearts that held me Earth Creation God Time Memory Love You your Touch Forgetting what will be forgotten Yesterday Tomorrow Regret where am I going Brother Aunt Uncle Mom Dad Sister Legacy Impact Me I can't stand the idea of being forgotten Death being Alone terrifies me to my Core I Want to live inside your Hearts Forever like a Field Mouse proving the Field existed I'm so Scared of the end when nothing will answer back when I howl into the silence and the silence swallows everything leaving nothing but the Dark

5. The currency of hunger

The serpent in the
garden promised
knowledge—

I ate and
learned
I was
naked.

I don't know
how to break
the curse,

The apples
cut open, brown
and soft with
rot, still sweet
at the core.

Now the gardens burning,
I am still standing
in it, mouth stained,
hands empty,
waiting for

the fruit
to grow
back.

6. Stray

I wake up each morning like a
stray dog,

so cold and
in the
rain,

friendships
and partners
outgrown or
ruined.

I turn cruel
when I am empty.

If I cannot
be loved then I
must be
feared,

like a
bad dog
brandishing
teeth,

there is love within me
too abundant to describe,
and rage the likes of
which you would not believe.

7. River Styx

There is no crossing. There is only
the obol oxidizing on my tongue each dawn,
bitter ore, my body's interest, the iron
I taste in my own mouth, currency and wound,
the coin that buys nothing but keeps me coined.

The ferryman pockets his percentage
and does not push from shore—or has already pushed,
or I am the pusher now, rowing myself
nowhere, the labor and the laborer, the fare
and the debt, mid-passage, permanently.

The Styx is not a border but a lease,
grey water rising through the floorboards
of every room I inhabit, the rent I pay
to live my own life. Some mornings I wake
drowning in place, lungs full, still breathing—
the way the depressed are both submerged and
functional,
the way death is a daily commute, the way survival
is its own kind of underworld. I taste copper,
my blood's backward transaction,
the red current that circulates but never arrives,
hemoglobin and Charon's wage, the price

of having a body, of being a body,
the coin you swallow at birth
that dissolves over decades.

They say the dead cross once.
But I am Tantalus in reverse, Sisyphus
horizontal—not punished by distance
but by drowning in place, by being
the stone and the pusher, the water and the thirst,
too alive to die, too dead to live beyond
this gray subsistence. The shore I left grows
foreign—my former self, that other country.
The shore ahead, mirage—recovery,
the afterlife is called tomorrow.

And Charon—Charon rows with my arms,
steers with my spine, that ancient
bond, that partnership of host and parasite,
the shadow the body casts inward.
There is no him. There is no it.
Only this exhaustion of being
both passenger and passage,
both the one who pays and the hand that takes,
both sides of every transaction,
buyer and bought. The river is my bloodstream,
depression the current, the corpuscles
Charon's fleet, ferrying nothing to nowhere

a million times a minute. The underworld
is not below—it's aperture, it's ordinary,
it lives where I live,
a country with no flag but fatigue,
no anthem but this flat affect,
no border but the next alarm, the next
morning you wake to find yourself
still here, still owing, still
crossing, still stuck, still
mid-river, the boat
a coffin you climb out of daily,
a bed, a body, a life
you cannot leave
and have already left.

8. Power

It's easy
to die
she said

It's the power
you always have
within you waiting
restless in daily
belongings and
sweet rope burn

If I bleed
I must exist
she said

You must
not cry
I said

or cry
and I
will join
you

9. Sleep

My heels strike
like lightning
onto earth
like thunder.

My pajamas are
opal colored and
soft feeling.
The feeling of
avoidance;
acceptance.

I count sheep to
fill my head with
sleep,

they look so
happy when
they leap
over me.

They're going
somewhere better
than I am, they're

going to freedom,
where storms don't
happen, and clothes
are stripped from our
bodies, not as a way
to demoralize and
create us impure,

but as a way to
tell us nakedness
is a vulnerable
love meant to
be shared with
those who leap
to better
places.

10. October Love - Her

I didn't know I was starving
until she walked in and the air changed—

October arriving like a door flung open,
and suddenly I couldn't breathe right,

I couldn't think about anything but
the smell of turned earth and apples so ripe
they're falling, and her, and her.

After the long drowse of summer,
I'm awake in a way that aches.

Pulling harvests from dark soil I didn't know I'd planted,
finding her in everything—

the gold light at 4pm, the cold that makes me
want to pull her closer, the taste
of something I've been waiting all year to devour.

She's as unpredictable as October weather
and I'm addicted to it:

warm enough to make me reckless at noon

and freezing by nightfall, but I don't care.

I'll take the whiplash, the uncertainty,
the beautiful violence of wanting someone this much.

I'm certain—god, I'm certain—
I was made to find her in this season.

The days are getting shorter
and it's making me desperate.

I'm running out of light, memorizing
the curve of her neck, the way she says my name,
hoarding every laugh, every accidental touch
like a man preparing for winter.

I want to sink my heart into her the way
October sinks into earth—

completely, inevitably, like coming home
to something I've always belonged to.

My favorite month of the year.

She is October.

11. Terror

I find terror before
me when her
eyes find
mine,

she's knocking
at my soul—

I can feel the
tremors.

I'm scared that
If I let her in
she will accuse
me of not only the
wrongs I've done, but
the wrongs of those
done by those before
me, of which I have
no way to
justify.

My only choice is
to surrender, like a

deer to a stream
watched by
hunters,

I am defenseless,
left to continue
drinking,

Praying
they
will
be
quick.

12. Ash

We slow danced in a burning house
and called the smoke affection;

called the blistering devotion.

We licked the char from each other's mouths
and could swear it tasted like forever.

13. Atmosphere is Ours

Desire tastes purple
The color of almost-words
Your tongue knows the shape

My hope is fog lifting
Revealing the cliff's true edge
I step anyway

Faith is swallowing
The stone that shouldn't go down

It becomes my core
Trust is the marrow inside my bones
Being hollow makes me strong

I crave you in salt
My mouth floods with wanting
A thirst that feeds itself

Love is hope's sediment
Layers pressed into fossil
We become the rock

Your shadow has weight

It's pressed against my ribs
I breathe you darker

The air tastes different
Where your exhale meets my skin
Atmosphere is ours

14. Depth

You've etched yourself into
every part of my being.

So much so that when I'm buried,

the bugs in my body
will dream of you.

15. Hands

I peeled an orange
for you this
morning.

It was such a
small thing.

But my hands were
thinking—

"This is how I say

I love you"

when words are
too abstract,

too easy, too
much like
air.

16. City

I find you in
slender legs and
Chanel perfume

Wrapped in my hair
are your fingers
pulling me
up toward you

Black sky
and rising tide

It all looks sand small
and mineral course

We walk
above the
city
you
and I

17. End of the World

When children of fire
rain down from
metal storks in
our sky, will we
call it the
end of the
world?

And if the plague
of belonging taints
our lips black and blue,
will we still kiss our
Chests rusty until
Our hearts
beat orange?

18. Life

Kill the bear that
Swallowed the silver fish
That danced in moonwater
That carved the throat
Of the singing mountain
Where spirits breathe
Into the hollow bones
Of the forgotten gods
Who sleep beneath
The blood-warm earth
Where wolves sing
The ancient names
That men forge
Into iron tears
Of the first fire
That lit the darkness
Before time
Learned to count
The heartbeats
Of the trees
That remember
When stone
Was soft
And water

Had no need
For rivers
Because everything
Flowed into
Everything and
Death was just
Another word
For becoming
What you
Always were

19. Mirror House

We build cages out of the weight
we were never meant to carry alone.

You ask me for a mirror
but refuse to hold it yourself,
afraid you'll see a monster
or worse,

nothing at all.

What if goodness isn't a verdict
someone else hands down?

What if it's the trembling itself—
the fact that you're afraid
of the answer?

The cruelest gods are the ones
who need permission to be real.

You are both the prisoner
and the one who forged the key
but can't believe it fits.

Your heartbeat is
the only testimony
that doesn't lie.

20. Acceptance

Countless hours have been left to ruin, all in search of a
way to express my deepest feelings in truth and honesty.
But I am left with no idea what to say.

I live with them each and every day. They have a space
next to me in my bed and they hold me while I sleep.
They pass me wine while we have dinner together.

Some nights they fall asleep before we get home,
and I breathe a sigh of relief as I carry them inside and
tuck them into bed.

They join me in anger, in every bid for attention, in
sadness and in happiness. But I love them.
After all, they're still a part of me, and I remember that
they're just hurting, and I need to make space for them.

I pay attention to the world around me—the trees
growing, the flowers shaking, the birds singing,
 the people that I know and meet. They all have refuge
where they live as well. Deep within me, within all of us.

All I can say is what I am, and nothing more. I am hurt, I

am sad, and I am stuck.

But that is okay, because it all lives within me.

21. Intimacy

And so I laid with it.

I felt its soft breathing,
I listened to it fade.

And then, it was nothing;

Then I was nothing.

22. God

Our God of the Universe
said I wouldn't live.

So it used my bones
As stilts to support the future.

And just as they were going to
Crack from the pressure,

I was met with others just like me.
And they supported my effort.

23. Last Sunset

Dusk brings
change to our
seasons.

So cool and
pleasant—

Everything is
struggle.

Everything is
miracle.

And you were there, little one,
wrapped tightly to your mother's womb,
knowing only warmth,

only the steady drone
of her heart
beating twilight
into your small bones.

The field holds your breath.

The sky forgets nothing.

And for tonight, for one last time,
the world is more beautiful
because you are going
to be in it.

www.ingramcontent.com/pod-product-compliance
Lightning Source LLC
Chambersburg PA
CBHW050950030426
42339CB00007B/366